BAAS Pamphlets in American Studies 12

AMERICAN PHOTOGRAPHY

D1273246

Mick Gidley

British Association for American Studies

First published 1983

© British Association for American Studies, 1983

ISBN 0 946488 02 9

The publication of a pamphlet by the British Association for American Studies does not necessarily imply the Association's official approbation of the opinions expressed therein.

ACKNOWLEDGEMENTS

For kindly providing good quality prints for us in this pamphlet, we are grateful to the staff of the following institutions: Center for Creative Photography, Univesity of Arizona, Tucson, Arizona; George Eastman House, Rochester, New York; Prints and Photographs Division of the Library of Congress, Washington, D.C.; The Museum of the City of New York; The Fine Arts Museum of San Francisco; The Whatcom Museum of History and Art, Bellingham, Washington. For permission to reproduce photographs here we would like to thank all of the above and, also, Exeter University Library; Instructional Resources Corporation, Laurel, Maryland; and the University of Washington Libraries, Seattle. In each case, the specific credit line requested is printed by the picture.

The author wishes to express his gratitude to certain friends and colleagues for helping to maintain his interest in American photography: James Enyeart, Tucson; Richard Maltby and Peter Quartermaine, Exeter; Robert Monroe, Seattle; Philip Stokes, Nottingham; Mike Weaver, Oxford; and, especially, Olaf Hansen, Frankfurt.

Printed by Peterson Printers, 12 Laygate, South Shields, Tyne & Wear. Tel: (0632) 563493

Contents

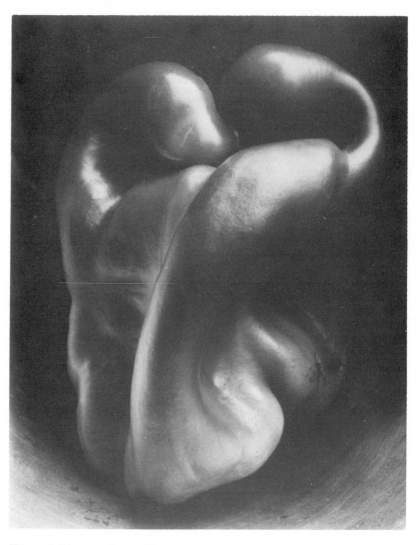

Edward Weston, *Pepper No.30*, 1930.

1: The Popular Art

Since the late sixties, throughout the economically advanced world but especially in the United States, there has been an extraordinary rise in mass interest in photography. Taking photographs is now the most popular hobby on earth. Temporary photographic exhibitions of all sorts are notably well attended. New permanent collections of photographs have been established, as at the Center for Creative Photography in Tucson, Arizona, and at the National Portrait Gallery in London. We have witnessed the commercial success — in fact the bestseller status — of innovative photo-documentary books like Michael Lesy's *Wisconsin Death Trip* (1973), with its juxtapositions of extracts from newspapers and fiction with previously little known Charles Van Schaik photographs made at the turn of the century. And photography is integral to both story and structure in such American novels as David Galloway's *A Family Album* (1978) and Paul Theroux's *Picture Palace* (1978).[1] Moreover, these new kinds of books are but a small tributary to the swollen river of more conventional photographic publications, both originals and reprints.

Inevitably, over roughly the same period, there has been quite widespread diffusion of ideas of photographic communication. Important questions have been asked — and variously answered — anew. What, precisely, is a photograph? What is the relationship between that part of the physical world framed by the camera and the actual photograph, between "reality" and "image"? Do photographs have a unique syntax or manner of structuring meaning? Can photographs be interpreted at all without a full knowledge of the context in which they were made and/or presented? Is there a sense in which the nature of a photographic image — though remaining physically more or less the same — may change with the passage of time?

The growing circulation — even popularization — of such questions owes much to Marshall McLuhan, especially his *Understanding Media* (1964), which spread many ideas about visual communication, including those of William M. Ivins.[2] Subsequently, Susan Sontag's essays in *The New York Review of Books* in the early seventies have become justifiably famous since their publication in her *On Photography* in 1977; and Roland Barthes' *Camera Lucida: Reflections on Photography* (1981), one of the final works of this major cultural critic and theoretician, has enjoyed comparatively large sales in the English-speaking world.[3] In such a climate, it is not surprising that the writings of even early photographic critics — including Americans like Sadakichi Hartmann — are being edited for contemporary readers, or that the history of photography itself is becoming more central as an academic field — in its own right, as part of art history, and as a legitimate concern of such subject areas as American Studies.[4]

It is certainly the case that much of of the sheer technological development of photography has taken place in the United States. Even before Louis Daguerre in France and William Henry Fox Talbot in England invented photography as such, many of the best magic lanterns were first patented by Americans. Daguerre had his precursors in the United States just as he had them in Europe, among them, Samuel F.B. Morse, the painter and celebrated inventor of telegraphy; and when the news of the Frenchman's success spread throughout the Western world in 1839, the relatively obscure Joseph Saxton soon took the earliest known American daguerreotype. Within only ten years a veritable photographic *industry* was under way and, in this sphere at least, the United States would not need to look overmuch to Europe again.

In 1850 William and Frederick Langenheim of Philadelphia made the first successful photographic lantern slides, thus ensuring that in towns and villages across the republic — and throughout the world — ordinary people in the mass could sit down together to see examples of the new medium. By 1851 there were at least fifty portrait studios in New York City alone and in 1853 the *New York Daily Tribune* estimated that three million daguerreotypes were being produced there that year. Stereoscopic cameras, and their resulting "three dimensional" images called stereographs, were first produced in Europe — on glass, then on paper — but caught on in an unprededented way in North America when improved upon and marketed by the Langenheim brothers in the late 1850s. The early, rather awkward and bulky stereoscopes for viewing and optically combining the two images on stereographs were considerably improved upon by the writer and doctor Oliver Wendell Holmes in 1859, and soon stereographs became a feature of every stable American home.[5] A further notable event was the successful effort of Eadweard Muybridge (born Edward Muggeridge, in England) to become the first person, perhaps as early as 1872, to photograph — under the watchful eyes of the West Coast railroad tycoon Leland Stanford — motion in series. Muybridge's bounding horses with all four legs off the ground and his humans engaged in numerous activities heralded the advent of the true record of motion itself that moving pitcures were to provide for the twentieth century.[6]

This catalogue of American innovation could be continued to at least 1961, when the polaroid process to achieve instant photographs was invented in the United States — or even to today and the production of cameras to take "three dimensional" pictures. But, from the perspective of cultural history, the single most significant American contribution was the opening of George Eastman's factory in Rochester, New York, in 1880. By 1888 Eastman had plagiarized the invention of celluloid for film patented by his compatriot, Hannibal Goodwin, and produced the first roll film in time to equip his new, inexpensive Kodak camera. It was this which made photography the first of the technologically advanced visual media to become a mass medium; as such, like film and television, its evolution may be seen as part — and as a symbol — of the country's ever increasing commitment to the mass production of consumer goods.

As with film and television later, the high technological development of photography was a facet of "Yankee know-how." Thomas Edison's efforts in refining cinematography and inventing the gramophone were simply parts of a career dedicated to improving industrial processes. The development by Eastman of a series of increasingly cheaper and simpler Brownie cameras was of the same order; as the company's slogan promised, "You push the button, we do the rest." Thus, in one of those ironies typical of American capitalism, Eastman became a millionaire and millions of Americans (and, in due course, others) were able to record the details of their daily lives: photography as the most democratic of all the arts was born.[7]

It is precisely aspects of the medium like these that have most excited some of its American practitioners and proponents. Paul Strand — himself a major figure in art photography — once wrote, for example, that American artists, unlike Europeans, should have no fear of "the new God, the Machine," but should positively exploit all its resources. The camera, a small machine, was, he thought, an appropriate means of expression for a people attuned to the modern era.[8] Such beliefs contributed to the formation of an approach to photography which, if not uniquely American, was distinctively so. It was an approach in which the mechanical nature of the camera was fully accepted and its use virtually proclaimed by the qualities of the resultant photographs: recognisable and sharp images, unmanipulated, and taken directly, head on, as it were. This is the so-called "straight" tradition that has dominated American photography.

The correspondence between streamlined production lines, vastly increasing mass consumption, modernity, and photography explains why the medium has been so important in — and for — the United States. Of course, the same is now true of Japan: whereas in postwar European cartoon imagery the American was the one typically identified by the possession (along with a big cigar, crew cut, spectacles and Bermuda shorts) of at least one camera, now a similar iconography is employed to signify the Japanese businessman on vacation. This similarity between the United States and Japan may suggest the dominance of economic over geographical factors in the determination of culture. But this particular cultural pattern is one which was first traced in the United States, at a period of critical transformation in her history; and, as a consequence, photography has probably had a more profound effect there than anywhere else.

Photography, cinema and television were all invented by Europeans, not Americans. Yet, as C.W. Ceram wrote, "What matters in history is not whether certain . . . discoveries take place, but whether they take effect."[9] In this pamphlet we shall make a series of probes to discover how photography took effect in three spheres: firstly, the social exploitation of photography and its role in transmitting cultural values; secondly, its use for purposes of deliberate — even official — documentation of the American scene in the twentieth century; thirdly, its employment as an artistic medium, both tributary to other arts and as a fine art in its own right. Throughout we shall see that interpreting the role of photography is complicated by difficulties and complexities arising from the very nature of the medium itself — by, indeed, the basic questions to be asked about the nature of photographic communication everywhere.

2: Mirror Images

The high degree of American technological activity in photography is mirrored in the social exploitation of the medium. The potentialities of the new medium were so quickly appreciated that soon thousands of photographs were being taken, for countless different commercial, official and personal reasons; and those that have survived provide a priceless resource for anyone interested in recapturing the American past, the experience of a society expanding, industrializing, transforming. These photographic records help us visualise the physical details, the precise environment of everyday life and historical achievement, but they also tell us much more. Since, as Conor Cruise O'Brien wrote, "The whole imaginative and intellectual life of a culture is one interacting field of force,"[10] photographs are shot through with cultural presumptions which can be difficult to decipher, but reveal much about the mind of the photographer, his employers, and the people who viewed what he had created.

Albums of American Life

As early as 1843 Edward Anthony set out to exploit the new medium by photographing all the members of Congress. His contemporary, the ubiquitous Matthew Brady, began in 1845 to collect photographic portraits of notable figures of his time, some of which appeared in his *Gallery of Illustrious Americans* (1850). In 1851 Brady made a prize-winning entry in the Great Exhibition at the Crystal Palace in London and, over a decade later, Abraham Lincoln could quip, "Matthew Brady and the Cooper Union speech made me President." Even before Brady's little army of photographers set out more or less systematically to "cover" the Civil War, the first photographs of war anywhere were made of episodes in the Mexican-American War of 1848. The volume and variety of the Civil War pictures contrast with the fascinating but more haphazard photographic coverage of the Crimean War by the enterprising Englishman Roger Fenton.[11]

Less dramatically, quite ordinary men made daguerreotypes of the California gold rush in 1848; an unknown photographer captured Caesar, the last slave owned in New York; a New York policeman started the first photographic rogues gallery or mug shots in 1858; E.A. Hegg made a comprehensive album of the scramble for gold in the Klondike; Darius Kinsey spent a lifetime recording the gigantic trees and the logging industry of the Pacific Northwest from the turn of the century onwards (*see the photograph on the front cover of this pamphlet*); and in 1912 E.J. Bellocq did a series on New Orleans prostitutes that eventually provided inspiration for Louis Malle's film *Pretty Baby* (1977).[12] And, on an even less official and exalted plane, ordinary Americans were able, through the availability of cheap cameras and because of their relative affluence, to photograph each other on an unprecedented scale. Thus it is that a vast mass of photographic documents of American life have come into existence — pictures of "common people" already forgotten by the wider world, of places and things to hand, and mostly snapped by someone anonymous.

We may learn much from studying such photographs, as collected in modern compilations like, for example, the American Heritage book, *American Album*.[13] We can gaze into the toothless faces of two elderly sisters, at the contented look of a plain woman surrounded by her five children, at the pert grin of a saloon girl — faces, expressions and, perhaps, stereotypes that the light of a century ago preserved. It is possible to follow the varieties of taste and necessity in dress, hairstyles, beards and moustaches through years, regions and occupations: an Eastern city gent with a carnation in his mouth, a bearded blacksmith whose hammer is forever prepared to strike sparks from the shoe on his anvil, a prospector and a gunman with the tools of their trades in their fists, or a group of pioneer Nebraskans showing us the watermelon they were about to eat — even the cards they held for poker that afternoon. There are photographs presenting a range of jobs in great detail: a lady corset manufacturer surrounded by her wares; a Western telegraphist, his little machine on a box at the foot of a telegraph pole, an armed escort around him, in the middle of a vast emptiness; a woman stenographer in an office otherwise reserved for men; and, of course, the omnipresent photographer himself, with his horse-drawn dark room, his massive camera, and his air of seeming to know what he is about. And there are people's amusements — a family musical group, early pin-ups, a river baptism, a balloon meet, a saloon by a lake in the middle of nowhere bearing the legend "Ladies without bloomers are not allowed on the beach."

As well as people, *American Album* provides us with houses — the sod houses of pioneers contrasted, for example, with the cluttered living rooms of the Eastern seaboard — and with places, buildings, structures. Some of these have now vanished utterly (such as small Western townships), some have changed beyond all recognition (like the Cincinnati waterfront), and some are preserved at a pivotal moment (Brooklyn Bridge newly opened, the Capitol or the Flatiron Building under construction, a court out West still situated in a tent). Then again, there is the land itself — forest, prairie, desert, mountain, river, lake and tilled field — and the original inhabitants of that land, the Indians. The book presents, in short, visions of a land, a nation, an era, and conveys much about the great mass of people who, as John Kouwenhoven has expressed it, lacked "the habit of scribbling."[14]

Although the title *American Album* is appropriate, it probably seems more so than it is. For one thing, as readers and viewers, we usually have no idea just how representative the compilation is; there are so many thousands of surviving images that all our generalizations are bound to be based on a tiny selection. Another book, *The American Image*, for example, contains some two hundred photographs chosen from the *five million* in the National Archives.[15] Even if we were able to go through the National Archives for ourselves, we would almost certainly be swamped by this quantity of images; indeed, serious research will have to be devoted to finding ways of categorizing images into groups limited enough to analyse. An even more serious problem with compilations of this sort is that they usually do not — and, often, cannot — give the context for each image reproduced; in other words, while the images are undoubtedly "documents of American life," it is not certain precisely *what* they document. Lavishly designed and bound, they can all too easily present the point of view — often a nostalgic one — held by their present-day compilers towards past eras.

How far are our responses, and the visions the photographs conjure up for us, the same as those possessed by those bygone people themselves? The vastness of America means that even today, in these times of easy travel, most Americans have a visual image of the country, perhaps even a national self-image, formed via the camera — television, the cinema, and, of course, photography. And before relatively cheap travel, this was even more so; people *had* to rely on pictures. Moreover, before photography, the connection between physical reality and picture was definitely more tangential. As Robert Weinstein and Larry Booth put it, "Consider this: in the nineteenth century, let us say 1825, a Maine fisherman had no convincing notion of what his fellow citizen in Kentucky truly looked like."[16] Unreliable prints of paintings and drawings of the West were widely distributed through the Eastern states, and Currier and Ives purveyed thousands of lithographs of genre views of American life around the nation. Photographs, as lithography developed technologically and aesthetically in the hands of such men as Francis D'Avignon, came more and more to fulfil this transmission function. Most of the official government surveys, for example, employed a photographer, sometimes of the quality of William Henry Jackson or Timothy O'Sullivan, to show the influential folk back East the rock formations and enticing vistas of the Western lands.

The general public too saw these and other images in the great photographic displays at the various major expositions, like that of 1876. More importantly, many photographs were taken on stereoscopic cameras; stereocards in series with titles like "Tom Thumb & Wife," "The Civil War," "Alaska after the Gold Rush of 1898," "Niagara Falls," "American Whaling" and "American Industry" were sold in thousands. Their importance for us does not lie in their three-dimensional quality so much as in the fact that they often had captions (sometimes long ones) on the back and were specifically intended to instruct. Now, captions of any sort are interesting, for, as Roland Barthes has shown, captioning is always a complex business. Sometimes the caption is necessary — and, where it exists, usually crucial — to complete the meaning of the image. A good example of this is John C.H. Grabill's photograph titled "Villa of Brule: The Great Hostile Indian Camp on River Brule Near Pine Ridge, South Dakota," which he copyrighted in 1891. It depicts a large encampment of Indian tepees and, in the foreground, a group of ponies standing in and drinking from a river flowing just below the photographer's camera. It could be almost any nineteenth-century Plains Indian gathering were it not for the clue in the caption — "Great Hostile Indian Camp" — which has made it possible for historians to identify it as, literally, the last large gathering of Brule, Ogalala and other Sioux at the end of the Ghost Dance period and immediately after the notorious army massacre of Big Foot's band at Wounded Knee. In other words, this picture — taken by the same historically minded photographer who captured "The Last Run of the Deadwood Stage" in 1890 — testifies to the final free days of the Sioux nation, for soon afterwards they were encircled by General Nelson A. Miles and transported back to the reservation.[17]

A.J. Russell, *Promontory Point, May 10, 1869.*
Courtesy of the Instructional Resources Corporation, Laurel, Maryland.

Sometimes, though, the caption, as Barthes put it, "invents an entirely new signified which is retroactively projected into the image, so much so as to appear denotated there."[18] One popular stereocard depicts two Indians, one a boy with a bow and arrow, looking from the foreground of the image towards the horizon; there, a train steams across a high bridge that spans the canyon in which they stand. The stereocard carries the following printed caption: "A Wonder to the Primitive Inhabitants."[19] Without the caption there are a number of different ways to read the image itself: it could be said to speak of the coexistence of ancient, primitive ways and modern technology; or, of the train as an intrusion into the lives and habitat of an aboriginal people; or, again, of the train fitting more appropriately into the landscape than the people it supersedes; or . . . . The caption, that is, serves to *interpret* the image.

In the case of stereographs, which were mostly produced and distributed by commerical companies using photographs derived from a number of different photographers (sometimes within the same series), captions were rarely the work of the maker of the image itself. The caption writer himself was engaged in an act of image reading, interpretation, and — though there were maverick companies and caption writers — the resultant captions usually present what is likely to have been the preferred reading of the culture of the time. All told, pictures like this — image plus caption — provided not so much formal information as an education in and reinforcement of the cultural values of the time. It could even be argued that many of the stereocard series should be seen — and analysed — as examples of self-instruction in Americanism.

An obvious instance of pictorial transmission of cultural values is to be found in another frontier photograph. On May 10, 1869, the tracks of the Union Pacific and Central Pacific Railroads met at Promontory Point, Utah. A golden spike was driven in to celebrate the achievement: for the first time, the continent was joined end to end by a single means of transport. There are several widely reprinted photographs of the event, but the full, uncropped version of the most popular of them, by Andrew J. Russell, official photographer for the Union Pacific, shows a mass of jubilant figures clustered in front of, around, and on two engines which have steamed to a halt confronting each other: unity within competition or vice versa (*see opposite*). The faces in the crowd are too distant to be discerned as individuals and the viewer may at first think that this is solely because the photographer was keen to portray the sheer size of the crowd. But there is also a vast expanse of sky: clearly, the photographer retreated until he could just hold within the frame the stars and stripes which unfurls from a stick atop a telegraph pole to the right. So this feat of capitalist investment and civil engineering is an event of *national* significance, and was literally *seen* to be so. Not surprisingly, Walt Whitman — who may well have seen the photograph — wrote his epic "Passage to India" precisely to laud the pivotal nature of the event in the life of the nation.

In other words, American photography really was a kind of "mirror image" of American culture, as has been suggested by Richard Rudisill, among others.[20] There was a profound reciprocity between the way many specific episodes were viewed (seen, thought of, valued) and the way they were represented in photographs. A similar correspondence is also apparent at the general level. It may be merely a coincidence of chronology that most of the era of massive American expansion, marked both by the westward movement and by the influx of thousands of immigrants from Europe, took place within the era of photography; but it is not an accident that so many aspects of this expansion came before a camera lens.

Capturing the West

In the exploration and settlement of the trans-Mississippi West, the principal agents (after the mountainmen) deliberately employed photographers to record their activities — whether government explorers, army surveyors and fort builders, the manufacturers of wagons for the trails westward, the great railroads which connected the centres of population, or the ranchers who initially settled the intervening acres. Eventually, of course, professional photographers themselves, as individual enterpreneurs, began to set up shop in the

Edward H. Latham, *U.S. Indian Agency Blacksmith and Indian Assistant,*
c.1900.

Courtesy of the Photography Collection, University of Washington Libraries, Seattle.
*Latham was based for many years at Nespelem on the Colville Reservation in eastern Washington
state, where many Nez Perces, including Chief Joseph, were exiled.*

new towns of the region and, finally, amateur photographers could
arise; as Susan Sontag said, "Faced with the awesome spread and
alienness of a newly settled continent, people wielded cameras as a
way of taking possession of the places they visited."[21]

Thus it was that men like J.K. Hillers could photograph "all the
best scenery" on the second descent of the Colorado River with John
Wesley Powell's 1871 expedition, that W.H. Illingworth could depict
the line of General Custer's expeditionary force entering the Black
Hills in 1874 (one of the events which triggered the fateful Battle of the
Little Bighorn two years later), that Russell and others could portray
the ceremonies at Promontory Point, that F.M. Steele could capture
cowboy life on the trail at the turn of the century, or that Edward H.
Latham, a United States Indian Service doctor by profession, could
take the likeness of a reservation blacksmith and his Indian assistant
(*see above*).[22]

It was almost inevitable that magnificent Western landscapes
would be produced — and they were, by Hillers, Muybridge, and

many others. A good deal of the processing then had to be done in the field; for instance, before the advent of the dry plate in about 1877, the view camera's massive glass negatives had to be evenly coated with chemical, then exposed and developed while still wet. For this reason there is particular poignancy in O'Sullivan's 1868 depiction of his own photographic wagon isolated on an enormous sand dune in the Carson Sink, Nevada.[23] Carleton Watkins, in 1861, was one of the first people to train a camera on the extraordinary geological formations to be found in what is now Yosemite National Park. And he was so successful that his views of such landmarks as El Capitan, Sentinel Dome and Bridal Veil both set the standard for others, such as Muybridge, and — because of their popularity with both the public and critics — became virtually *the* definitive Yosemite views. In 1884 F.J. Haynes was appointed "Official Photographer of Yellowstone National Park." This enabled him to establish a summer studio there and to produce a flow of images which, like Watkins' of Yosemite, established a visual awareness nationally of the country's first National Park.

This tradition has continued almost to the present in the person of Ansel Adams. Adams has made countless pictures of Yosemite, held an annual summer workshop there for many years, and in 1946 received a Guggenheim Fellowship to make National Park views. One of the finest of his National Park pictures is "The Tetons, Thunderstorm" (1942), with the jagged Teton Mountains towering above a superb curve of the silver-lit Snake River. Another — his striking 1944 image of "Moonrise, Hernandez, New Mexico" — has become so revered that, in its original print form, it has fetched more money at auction ($71,000) than any other photograph to date.[24]

Photographers like these both recorded aspects of the West and, consciously or unconsciously, created an iconography of it that has retained its potency, especially as replicated in the Western film. For instance, W.H. Jackson's famous image titled "North from Berthoud Pass" (1874) has little to say about the specific geographical nature of Berthoud Pass, but it is a classic evocation of westering man; the figure moving off into the unknown even wears a hat that could be mistaken for a tricorn hat of the Revolutionary War era as if he is a kind of founding father obeying the injunction of his nation's "manifest destiny" to subdue the alien and awesome continent.[25]

The camera's portrayal of Indians is particularly susceptible to this kind of analysis. Of the several important photographers of Native Americans, including Adam Clark Vroman, the most enterprising was Edward S. Curtis. Curtis and his assistants made both a photographic and written record of over eighty different peoples west of the Mississippi who "still retained some semblance of their

Edward S. Curtis, *The Fire Drill-Koskimo*, 1914.

Courtesy of the Library, University of Exeter.
In this photograph of a Kwakiutl fire maker the movement of lines and the play of features in the foot of the tree, in the man's apparel, in the twigs in his hair, in the very lines of his face, all betoken that he is as rooted in the land as the tree by which he squats.

traditional ways of life" at the last moment at which it was possible to do so, thus creating *The North American Indian* (1907-30), a publication of twenty volumes of illustrated text accompanied by twenty portfolios of photogravures. Curtis' Indians are usually represented as deeply spiritual, totally at one with their environment, and at some still point in the circle of their lives (*see above*); often the people in these images are so composed as to seem in a different dimension to the bustle of this world — to be, in effect, simultaneously, above the flow of time, redeemed, and also static, ossified into a pre-evolutionary state and, therefore, already vanished, so to speak, from the earth.[26]

How The Other Half Lives

When, mainly in the East, photographers confronted the alien multitudes of immigrants, the tenements of the increasingly teeming cities and working conditions in the aggressive new industries, a complex process of image-making occurred similar to that in the Far West. Two people in particular devoted significant portions of their lives to recording, and commenting upon, these urban phenomena — Jacob A. Riis and Lewis Hine.

Riis was himself an immigrant, born in Denmark, who had lived through a period of hardship after his arrival in 1870 in the United

States. He became a crime reporter for New York newspapers and very quickly came to see poverty and slum conditions as major causes of crime. He wielded a deft pen in articles that emphasized not social analysis but stories of individual tragedies. With the help of Theodore Roosevelt, first as head of the police board and later as Governor of New York and President, Riis mounted a vigorous campaign for housing reform. He believed that the way to get reform was by arousing people to the facts. "The power of fact," he wrote in *The Making of an American* (1900), "is the mightiest lever of this or any day." And, as Alexander Alland said, "he saw in the photograph a supreme weapon of fact."[27]

The first appearance of some of his pictures, in 1889, as the basis for line drawings in *Scribner's* magazine, led to immediate demand for a whole book: *How the Other Half Lives* (1890), the first American account of social conditions to be documented by half-tone pictures made from photographs. In it there were pictures of homeless boys sleeping rough, teenage gangs in their "dens," cigarmakers, tailors and others working in tenement homes, people living in windowless cellars or crowded in attics, overfilled lodging houses, and the like. For the next ten years or so Riis used images such as these as lantern-slide illustrations for extremely popular lecture tours around the nation.

Riis' efforts and photographs were certainly rewarded: notorious slums were knocked down, sanitary settlements were built, New York City's water supply was purified, and Riis himself became perhaps the best-known reformer of his generation. Some of the pictures possess a naked kind of force, the power of directness: all these people do, indeed, sleep in this small space. But it is important to realise that there is a strong voyeuristic element about them. In such famous images as "Mullen's Alley, Cherry Hill" (*see the centre spread*), the people photographed are separated from the viewer (and the photographer) by a largish expanse of empty foreground space and are caught, so to speak, at the opening of a dead-end alley; in visual terms, they are The Poor, "the other half." Such an impression is at one with what is known of Riis' photographic methods and — though in artistic terms he was not conscious of it — his fundamental ideology. Many of his images were made at night, with flash; sometimes his sleeping subjects would be actually awakened by the sudden blaze which exposed their miserable quarters, and he was able to enter many "criminal" haunts precisely because he was a police reporter accompanied by a policeman. Riis "voiced no protest against the arrangement of society which consigned masses of men to mean lives," wrote the perceptive historian Robert Bremner. "His was no cry for social justice, but a call to the propertied classes to bestir themselves lest the crime engendered in the slums . . . invade [their] comfortable quarters."[28]

In the past the efforts of Riis and Lewis W. Hine have sometimes been crudely yoked together. Certainly both wanted to modify the cultural attitudes of the American viewing and reading public, but their approaches, techniques and impact were significantly different. Hine was a sociologist and reformer who, like Riis, certainly wanted his photographs — whether on posters, in books, pamphlets or magazines — to move people and produce change. When he began, in 1904, he was especially concerned to document the conditions under which some two million American children had to work; in the first decade of the century he photographed hundreds of immigrants as they suffered the humiliations, hopes and traumas of being processed through Ellis Island; and during his later career he made graphic images for his book *Men at Work* (1932), including vertigo-inducing views of the construction of the Empire State Building.[29]

Several of Hine's photographs introduce the concept of "fictional space"; in "Dannie Mercurio, Washington, D.C." (1912), for example, Dannie, a newsvendor, "moves" towards the viewer on a line of paving stones while a comfortably off woman moves away from him at right angles. The fact that the frame also contains the woman — and in the background, a couple of roadways at oblique angles to each other — allows the picture to be read as cultural information, even news: the ways of the haves and the have-nots, the old and the young, even the past and the present, are diverging. Or again, consider his 1905 image, "Madonna of Ellis Island" (*see the centre spread*): a woman with Mona Lisa features holds a baby on her lap while a slightly older child gazes adoringly at the baby; the background to this trio consists of a huge arc of glass and steel, but is also subtly reminiscent of cathedral stained glass. Clearly, this is an image which can only be fully appreciated if its symbolic connotations are borne in mind.

In other words, despite the fact that Hine took many thousands of photographs and that he sometimes used flash (as he did in most of his Ellis Island pictures, including his "Madonna" study), there is little or nothing of the voyeuristic in his work. His portrait subjects look into the camera and seem to seek interaction with the viewer as fully dignified human beings, however poor or exploited. Even when this is not quite the case — in, say, the depictions of young girls prematurely aged, by malnutrition and heavy labour, or whose spines have been permanently twisted by attention to demanding machines — there are often signs of their humanity within the frame. In "Lucy and Savannah, Gastonia, North Carolina" (1908), for example, the two wizened-face girls have proudly donned their Sunday best for the picture. Even in "Mental Institution, New Jersey" (1924) the two monstrous children are seen deferentially, as it were, from a slight distance, and in profile; Barthes has claimed that the point in this picture which really pricked *his* consciousness was not at all the disabilities of the children but the boy's old-fashioned "Danton collar, the girl's finger bandage."[30]

Thus, in the best of Hine's pictures the viewer has to be an active participant in their interpretation if anything like their full meaning is to be liberated. This is a result partly of his ideological position and partly of his conscious artistry. He himself came in his later life to call his work "interpretive photography." For instance, he surrounded his picture with the information of which, in a sense, they are part: statistics, polemical argument, narrative, other pictures; in the case of the studies taken for the National Child Labor Committee, the viewer thus confronts, say, this particular child in the cottonmill *and* the greed of industry for maximum profit which demands her employment *and,* in all likelihood, his own passive acquiescence in the practice. The viewer is encouraged, that is, not just to see, but to *be* a witness.

Despite their differences, in both Riis and Hine there was an urge to document insufficiently regarded areas of American life, to create an undeniable record; both, but especially Hine, did so with a conscious awareness of the artistic potentialities of the medium. In that respect they were typical of almost all those involved subsequently in the deliberate documentation of American society by means of photography.

3: Visual Documents

The urge to document the realities of American life predated the efforts of Riis and Hine. Photographers of the Far West had been inspired by such an ambition, and had been encouraged by the organizers of exploration and enterprise in the West, including even government officials. Eadweard Muybridge, according to some authorities, was "Official Photographer for the U.S. Government for the Pacific Coast" — and if he did not hold such a title, he certainly worked freelance for several government departments. In the twentieth century several more ambitious and systematic projects have been undertaken, usually with corporate or official support, all of them designed to observe and record some aspect of American life, many of them significant for their exploitation of the medium. The most ambitious and influential remains the government-sponsored project launched under the aegis of the New Deal.

The FSA — and Photojournalism

Soon after coming to power in 1933, Franklin D. Roosevelt appointed Rexford Tugwell, a professor of Economics at Columbia University, to be his Assistant Secretary of Agriculture. The sufferings of farmers in the agricultural depression of the 1920s became almost catastrophic in the the years following the 1929 stock market crash. In 1933 emergency programmes started to channel money to farmers in distress, some of which evolved into the Resettlement Administration, with Tugwell as its administrator. He appointed a junior colleague at Columbia, Roy E. Stryker, as head of the Historical Section. In 1934 Stryker hired the first photographers, including one of his former graduate students, Arthur Rothstein.

Over the years the Photographic Unit suffered many bureaucratic and political switches and changes. In 1936 the Resettlement Administration was established at the Department of the Interior, then in December it was moved to the Department of Agriculture and, in 1937, became the Farm Security Administration. Sometimes the funds were so low that only two photographers (usually Rothstein and Russell Lee) could be retained, whereas in more prosperous times the complement was six, even eight. Occasionally the economics of the operation dictated that photographers be seconded to (and paid by) other institutions — Rothstein went to government filmmaker Pare Lorentz, for instance, Walker Evans to *Fortune* magazine and several others to the Tennessee Valley Authority. By 1937 Tugwell was considered "too radical" and was forced to resign. In the late thirties various accusations were voiced: the FSA issued too much "government propaganda," the Unit's pictures were "too depressing," and so on. In 1941 the Unit was merged with the Office of War Information and many of its photographers were drafted. Stryker strove, as always, to keep it going, but, in a wartime atmosphere which encouraged the depiction of what William Dean Howells had termed the "smiling aspects of life," its future was limited. Also, certain commercial photographic agency people viewed the extensive FSA files as a rival source of pictures and actually wanted them destroyed. Fortunately, Stryker was easily able to persuade the poet Archibald MacLeish, then Librarian of Congress, to take them, in 1943, into the Library's care. There they remain, a resource for the foreseeable future. Stryker went on to teach and, more important, to continue his work in the field of photographic documentation, but this time for industry and big business.[31]

The particular conception and range of the FSA Photographic Unit's activities had several sources, some of which were related to Stryker's own personality and interests. He was certainly aware of Brady's efforts to record the earlier national tragedy of the Civil War and he was probably aware of Curtis' massive Indian undertaking. He had enjoyed personal friendships with Hine and Margaret Bourke-White, who reached the height of her fame as a *Life* photographer in the thirties and collaborated with her then husband, novelist Erskine Caldwell, on such deliberate efforts to arouse the public conscience as *You Have Seen their Faces* (1937).[32] He was responsible for acquiring all the pictures — including many by Riis and Hine — for *American Economic Life and the Means of its Improvement* (1925), a book by Tugwell and Thomas Munro. At the onset of the Depression Tugwell and Stryker were thinking about a book to be called "A Pictorial Source Book of American Agriculture"; in a sense, this was a project that the FSA files could realise. As its first title indicates, the chief aim of the FSA was the resettlement of farmers of limited means, through very low interest loans, on more productive, economically viable farms. The FSA was also concerned to resettle farmers in purpose-built suburban developments and subsistence housing on communal farms — the latter a controversial issue, as was the FSA's provision of government camps for migrant workers. The FSA was also involved in large-scale conservation programmes, in the fight against erosion and for more forestation. At first, all the Historical Section's photographs were intended to document the work of the Administration — its procedures, its clients, its problems and, of course, its successes. Thus Rothstein would produce works like "A model community planned by the suburban division of the US Resettlement Administration: Interior of a house," taken in Greenbelt, Maryland, in November 1936.

But Stryker realised that more was possible. For a start, his own background in agriculture and economics made him want the photographers to get at underlying conditions and causes. He was ready, therefore, to be influenced by others whose ideas were more far-reaching. One such figure was Robert Lynd, author of the famous sociological study *Middletown* (1929). "Shooting scripts" were evolved with such instructions as this: "Pictures which emphasize the fact that the American highway is often a more attractive place than the places Americans live. 'Restless America' Beautiful Highways . . . Elm, or maples at the curve of the road . . . Lunch Rooms and Filling Station Truckers stopped to eat . . . Trailers on Road . . . People walking on road . . . ."[33] This may give the impression that there was a typical FSA (or Stryker) picture, but such is far from the case. There may have been *ideal* Stryker images; John Collier, an FSA photographer during the very last phase of the Unit's life, remembered that Stryker once told him to get a picture of "the smell of burning Autumn leaves."[34] But, in actual day-to-day operation, the scripts and instructions served primarily as an invitation to the photographers to use their own eyes, *to interpret* what they saw.

And this was just as well, since some of the photographers were fully mature artists with ideas of their own and others, though essentially trained on the job, like Collier and Gordon Parks, were strong characters concerned to forge personal styles. Dorothea Lange — often since considered *the* archetypal FSA photographer — had made studies of conditions for migrant workers before joining the Unit. Carl Mydans was an experienced journalist, and already skilled in the use of the relatively new, small format 35mm camera. Walker Evans, who at that time liked to take very considered images with a large-view camera, was sufficiently appreciated as an artist to have a show of his work at the Museum of Modern Art in New York in 1938 while he was attached to the FSA. Ben Shahn was already a significant painter and print-maker.[35] The fact that such people rubbed shoulders, so to speak, no doubt indicates that they could have influenced one another and some were much more prepared to try to please Stryker than others. But their own senses of themselves and the sheer mass of the pictures they took — over a quarter of a million — means that it is impossible, unproductive and absurd to isolate "typical" FSA images, whether Lange's famous portrait of an anguished "Migrant Mother" (1936), framed by the tousled heads of her children, or her "Hoe Culture" (*see opposite*), or one of Lee's views of the desperately poor, or Shahn's Black "Cotton Pickers" (1935), their enormous sacks trailing far behind them in the furrows, still to be filled.

There was always an artistic dimension to the FSA project. As well as Evans' "American Photographs" exhibition, FSA images were featured in other art shows, including Willard Morgan's "First International Exhibiton of Photography" (1938). Perhaps most important of all, they were used as the pictorial basis for a new form, the book-length photographic essay, such as *12 Million Black Voices* (1941) by Richard Wright and Edwin Rosskam, a work that is essentially an illustrated history of the role of Blacks in American history and society. Probably the most enduring of those publications — in that they have been reprinted for the benefit of succeeding generations — are MacLeish's *Land of the Free* (1938), which features his poetry as a "sound track" to the photographs, and *Let Us Now Praise Famous Men* (1941), the product of James Agee's collaboration with Evans for *Fortune*, a magnificent and idiosyncratic record in words and photographs of their sojourn with two families of Alabama sharecroppers.

It is somewhat harder, from a present-day perspective, to determine the precise impact of the FSA images during the existence of the Unit. Some were used in government reports issued by other agencies. Many, of course, were channelled to regional offices of the FSA itself and were used in brochures and booklets intended for FSA clients,

Dorothea Lange, *Hoe Culture. Sharecroppers, Eutah, Alabama,* 1937.

Courtesy of the Library of Congress.

There is an emphasis in this FSA picture on balance: two shorter figures either side and equidistant from a central one, two straw hats, two hoes going one way, the middle one the other. Lange also took the sharecroppers at just the angle that would obscure their faces, their individuality. They are anonymous, literally faceless. Hoe Culture *is an image of the formality of work.*

including numerous farmers with limited literacy. The pictures had to catch the attention of such readers. Increasingly they were also released to newspapers and magazines. Thus Rothstein's famous photograph of a man and a blond boy running for shelter from obliterating grey dust, his "Dust Storm, Cimarron County" (1936), and his views of drought-stricken land, and Evans' Mississippi flood pictures, were very widely circulated, reprinted, and seen. When Stryker could not prevent it, they appeared without credits to either the photographers or the FSA, but steadily this, too, was secured, not only in such regular and sympathetic outlets as *Survey Graphic* and *US Camera*, but also in the new mass-circulation illustrated journals, *Life* and *Look*.

There was, in fact, a strong interplay between the FSA Photographic Unit and the American development of that pervasive enterprise that we know as photojournalism, a genre virtually invented in the United States, which largely paralleled the rise, if not the ultimate fall, of these same picture magazines. This was especially so in the case of the so-called "humanists" or "concerned" photographers of the same generation and succeeding ones, men like W. Eugene Smith, Robert Capa, Bruce Davidson, and, to a lesser extent, Paul Strand and Robert Frank. If Smith may be taken as exemplary of their aims for a moment, their intellectual or vocational inheritance from Riis and the FSA is apparent; he spoke of the mass influence of

Jacob A. Riis, *Mullen's Alley, Cherry Hill,* c.1888.

Courtesy of The Museum of the City of New York.

". . . in visual terms they are The Poor, 'the other half'" (page 17).

Lewis W. Hine, *Madonna of Ellis Island,* 1905.

". . . this is an image which can only be fully appreciated if its symbolic connotations are borne in mind" (page 18).

photography, stressing that "it is important [that] the photographer-journalist have . . . a strong sense of integrity and the intelligence to understand and present his subject accordingly." Certainly, Smith himself could claim to have brought such qualities to his picture stories on the missionary and welfare work of Albert Schweitzer, on the Ku Klux Klan, or on the Japanese victims of chemical pollution.[36] Bruce Davidson's work was more laconic and ironic, especially the Harlem pictures collected in *East 100th Street* (1970). This book includes a picture of an apartment wall with a portrait of President Kennedy, honoured with homely decorations, juxtaposed against a window that opens on to a devastated empty lot; the little girl sitting on the window ledge is semi-naked, innocent, vulnerable, yet obviously lacking the future that the revered and decorated portrait symbolizes. This photograph is reminiscent of, and has a similar feel to, Robert Frank's "Parade, Hoboken, New Jersey" (1955), where the stars and stripes obscures the face of an anonymous woman standing in a window, failing to see out. This image appeared in a wide-ranging book of Frank's pictures introduced by Jack Kerouac, *The Americans* (1959), one person's view of the country, from quiet court-house squares in small towns to hostile teenagers, from segregated buses to a brass band at the 1956 Democratic party convention.[37]

As Susan Sontag has reminded us, the effect of such photographs does not remain stable, however high the moral integrity of the photographer. Speaking of Smith — though her words could well be applied to others — she wrote: "[The images] move us because they document a suffering which arouses our indignation — and distance us because they are superb photographs of Agony, conforming to surrealist standards of beauty."[38] With the passage of time indignation becomes inappropriate, and the image survives as an object of aesthetic rather than social or political contemplation. The reading of a photograph is a complex business, demanding that we seek to understand both the cultural and other values which surrounded it — and which it embodied — at the moment of its creation and the qualities, perhaps almost purely formal, which retain our attention.

Courts and Monuments

Since the demise of the FSA the notion of repeating its comprehensive undertaking has not died, but it has proved more of an inspiration than an actual model. Its closest rival, so to speak, was the Court House Project. Funded (on a very lavish scale) by the whiskey manufacturers, Joseph E. Seagram & Sons, Inc., directed by Phyllis Lambert and Richard Pare, and involving twenty-five photographers, the Court House Project was one of the largest architectural photographic enterprises ever undertaken. It was started in September 1974 with the intention of photographing a large proportion of the county court houses in the United States; by 1977 more than a third of the 3,043 buildings had been covered, thus creating a file of over eight thousand images and accompanying research correspondence, all of which was transferred to the Library of Congress as the Project wound itself up. In 1978 a travelling exhibition based on the project began to circulate and the book *Court House* appeared, complete with essays by the directors, by two architectural historians, and a Massachusetts Supreme Court justice.[39]

To some extent — in that it documents with one art an aspect of another art — the Court House Project may be thought of as a parallel to the Works Progress Administration's Index of American Design undertaken during the New Deal. In considering the Project from the photographic point of view alone, though, the significance of the pictures may be appreciated in three main spheres: architectural history, urban studies, and photographic art itself.

The Project made a fine record of buildings — many of them lesser known ones — by such major American architects as Henry Hobson Richardson, who very nearly established a national style in the late nineteenth century, and Frank Lloyd Wright. It brought to notice many buildings of architectural merit and interest in regions, such as Texas, which had been virtually ignored by architectural historians. And, because of its scope, it documented both the diffusion and limitations of certain styles, such as the neo-classic. Unlike state buildings — state capitols, governors' mansions, etc. — county court houses were built by people whose reference point was as local as the next county. Consequently, there is tremendous diversity in style and size. These buildings — with their land records, war memorials, registers of vital statistics, trial proceedings — are a monument to the particular aspirations, the economic status and aesthetic sense of people at specific times in their history. The photographs, therefore, often evoke such matters as, on one hand, the persistence of sectionalism or, on the other — in the rejection of the gothic style, for instance — a virtually national belief in the need to repudiate ecclesiastical associations in civic affairs.

Because the photographers captured court-house exteriors, even views from the steps, windows or domes, the pictures register in many cases the present-day decay of inner-city areas; the court house looks lost or abandoned. Or, in other instances, an old court house is surrounded by expensive and beautiful commercial buildings; clearly, it has retained its legal function while losing its civic or social purposes. Then again, of course, in numerous small towns it is possible to see that the court house is the *only* building with any distinction, the thing which makes this town stand out from a thousand others around the nation.

Architectural photography presents problems of its own, and the photographers commissioned by the Project — some of them veterans

William Clift, *Old St. Louis County Court House Reflected in the Equitable Building.*
William Clift, Seagram County Court House Archives. © Library of Congress.

like Paul Vanderbilt, most of them young and just emerging into prominence — attempted to solve them in ways most appropriate to themselves. Stephen Shore, for example, took numerous very still exteriors (and interiors) devoid of people which nevertheless, in their rich colour and/or significant detail, reveal the human imprint of the buildings' users. William Clift had, perhaps, the talent with the best range for the Project, and produced both marvellously atmospheric views of exteriors of relatively undistinguished buildings *and* sharply focussed details, whether a particular cast-iron design, one bend in a well-crafted stairway, or the display of cereal products exhibited in Bent County Court House, Las Animas, Colorado. His juxtaposition of the old and the new in his photograph of the old St. Louis County Court House reflected in a glass-walled modern business building (*see opposite*) is particularly striking.[40]

A comparable enterprise which was much less reverential towards its subject-matter was Lee Friedlander's dozen years of work — almost haphazard at first — towards his large-sized portfolio, *The American Monument*. Published in 1976, and not specifically intended to be a record as such, this prints two hundred and thirteen images selected from several thousand negatives made by Friedlander all over the United States and constitutes his "memorial in photographs to the American Monument."[41] There are statues of First World War doughboys, repetitive yet individual, from various parts of the nation; monuments to striking personalities in all walks of life, from a stone effigy of theatre impresario George M. Cohan idling in Times Square, New York, to Mary Dyer, Quaker, in Boston, to Emmanuel Swedenborg in Chicago, to Tom Mix, his lonely horse silhouetted against the sky, near Florence, Arizona; replicas of Liberty erected by local Boy Scout troops; alarmingly varied versions of national heroes, especially Lincoln; the frieze to Robert Gould Shaw and the First Black Volunteer Regiment that lay behind Robert Lowell's poem, "For the Union Dead" (1964); monuments to firemen, ambulance personnel, school children, sailors, Elks, Justice, and the Pony Express; numerous lone Confederate and Union soldiers; and set pieces from the Vicksburg and Gettysburg Civil War battlefields.

Many of these are, of course, seen head-on, but in the case of others there is the definite air of humour or irony that we might expect from the man who has elsewhere presented strangely disturbing portraits of himself and pictures of trees so arranged that we witness not the orderliness of the natural world, but a chaos of twisting branches, threatening twigs, or, in the case of "Yuma, Arizona" (1970), a lone tree which seems about to invoke a dust storm.[42] For example, Father Duffy, the jingoistic Catholic chaplain to New York troops in World War One, is depicted with the frame sufficiently enlarged to encompass the enormous Coca Cola sign and the fractured parts of other advertisements with which he is incongruously forced to share space in Times Square. Gutzon Borglum's enormous carvings of Lincoln, Jefferson, Washington and Theodore Roosevelt on the face of Mount Rushmore in South Dakota are presented as reflected from the plate glass of the viewing area below, with an overweight tourist couple occupying the foreground, oblivious of Friedlander's camera as they peer through binoculars and photograph the mountain. *The American Monument*, like the other visual documents treated here, is both a record and a vision.

4: An American Art

From the beginning of photography in the United States, some Americans had appreciated that this new means of visual communication could become a new art-form of great aesthetic potentiality. The first significant artistic achievement was that of the portrait makers, best known of whom was the prolific Matthew Brady. At about the same time, in Boston, the studios of Albert S. Southworth and Josiah Hawes were producing equally distinctive work. They made, for instance, a suitably imposing picture of the Massachusetts Chief Justice, Herman Melville's father-in-law, Lemuel Shaw (1851) and, about a year earlier, caught Harriet Beecher Stowe, author of *Uncle Tom's Cabin* (1852), in a surprisingly diffident pose.[43] Very many other major American writers, thinkers and doers of the nineteenth century — from John Quincy Adams and Edgar Allan Poe, through Asher Durand, the painter, and Lewis Cass, the politician, to Frederick Douglass, escaped slave and abolitionist leader — sat for notable camera portraits. Even reclusive Emily Dickinson and shy Nathaniel Hawthorne submitted for their likenesses, fascinated by the new medium. Hawthorne, in fact, was so interested that he made a daguerreotypist one of the chief characters of *The House of the Seven Gables* (1851). "While we give it credit only for depicting the merest surface," his Holgrave says, "it actually brings out the secret character with a truth that no painter would venture upon, even could he detect it."[44]

Walt Whitman, too, had a heightened awareness of the new medium. On the one hand, he could complain to Horace Traubel, "I have been photographed, photographed, photographed, until the cameras themselves are tired of me." On the other, after seeing the

Philadelphia Centennial Exposition of 1876, Whitman allocated photography (both image and commodity) the prime position in one of his lists, in his "Song of the Exposition": "The photograph, model, watch, pin, nail, shall be created before you." He called one set of his Civil War prose sketches "City Photographs," and so often his poems are overtly built on a series of exact visual impressions; for example, "Sparkles from the Wheel," or "Cavalry Crossing a Ford," with its "Behold the brown-faced men, each group, each person, a picture . . . ."[45] Many times Whitman called for the rise of American artists capable of recording scenes that he himself was witnessing on his travels. Photographic artists were soon to take up the challenge, and the photographic illustrations to his *Leaves of Grass* by Edward Weston, gathered on Weston's own travels throughout the nation in the late 1930s, may be seen as one of the fullest artistic responses to it.[46]

Other landscape photographers, too, have maintained this interaction with literature. For example, for the first two decades of this century Herbert Gleason meditated visually over Henry David Thoreau's Walden Pond near Concord, Massachusetts, and over other scenes of Thoreau's life and writings.[47] Novelist Wright Morris produced sharp, uncluttered Nebraska images for his own *The Inhabitants* (1946), and Art Sinsabaugh used huge "horizontal" shots of Middle West prairiescapes, most notably, as his counterpoint to a 1964 publication of some of Sherwood Anderson's *Mid-American Chants* (1918).[48] It could be argued — and Eliot Porter himself has insisted — that in Porter's still landscapes, bird studies and the like, especially those published by the conservationist Sierra Club, he consistently followed such Thoreauvian themes as "in Wilderness is the preservation of the world," even into the era of recent colour photography. In many of his pictures there is a delightful interplay between a tendency towards blocks of almost flat colour, as in an oriental print, and a reverence for the autonomous reality of individual objects, whether aspens quaking in the wind or a single leaf bearing caterpillars.[49]

However persistent the inspiration of literature, the fuller assimilation of photography to painting was only to be expected. For a start, painting seemed to provide a ready-made vocabulary. Thus, some of its generic categories — landscape, say, or portraiture — could be readily extended to contain the products of the newer medium. In fact, some nineteenth-century landscape photographers, including Carleton Watkins, influenced — and were overtly influenced by — landscape painting, especially works by members of the Hudson River School and their followers. This is pointedly so in the work of John Moran and Charles Beirstadt. Moran was the brother of Thomas Moran, the artist who accompanied W.H. Jackson on that first survey, the Hayden survey, of the Yellowstone area in 1871. Charles Bierstadt was painter Albert Bierstadt's brother and his widely circulated stereoviews of Niagara Falls may be profitably compared with Frederick Church's paintings of the Falls.[50] However, such interaction between painting and photography seemed to some people to make the new art subordinate to the older, more respectable medium, to deny the legitimacy, even the possibility, of art photography developing values, criteria, techniques or qualities of its own. Even more important, though, was the need to break the attitude that photography was primarily concerned with the accurate recording of the world around, and to destroy its subservience to everyday practical uses.

The Photo-Secession

The first significant American movement in art photography was the Photo-Secession, which began in 1902. As its name implies, it constituted a revolution in a number of ways. For its founder, Alfred Stieglitz, it was partly a declaration of independence from the group of largely amateur photographers who dominated the New York Camera Club (whose journal he had edited) in favour of the full-time professional pursuit of photography. To some extent, it was analogous to the British Linked Ring which, founded in 1893 (and including Stieglitz among its membership), stressed the "Brotherhood" of photographic artists. Like the painters and photographers of Germany who in their revolt against the Academy formed the Secession in 1898, Stieglitz wanted photography to be treated as one of the fine arts.

To this end, Stieglitz also founded the quarterly journal *Camera Work* (1903-17), which became one of the most influential little magazines the United States has produced. Besides literary and cultural commentary and reproductions of drawings, it published photogravures both by members of the group, such as Gertrude Käsebier, Edward Steichen, and Clarence H. White, and by important Europeans and newcomers, including Paul Strand, as well as critical articles by emerging aestheticians of the medium, like Charles H. Caffin and Sadakichi Hartmann. Equally important was the establishment by Stieglitz, with Steichen's assistance, of "the little galleries of the Photo-Secession" (1905-17) at 291 Fifth Avenue (later simply "291"). Here, not only were there major photographic exhibitions, but shows of work by artists (often innovative ones) in other media: Rodin, Marsden Hartley, John Marin, Matisse, Max Weber, Picasso, and Brancusi; in other words, it paralleled and reinforced the trends leading towards the liberation of American attitudes to art represented by the landmark Armory show of 1913.[51]

The kind of photography favoured by Stieglitz — indeed, exhibited by him at 291, at the major shows he organized in 1909 and 1910, and

and at his later galleries, The Intimate Gallery (1925-29) and An American Place (1929-46) — underwent a subtle but profound change in the course of his long career. At first he was concerned to champion "pictorial photography," by which was then meant photographs which had no advertising, commercial, social, or informative purpose, but were complete pictures unto themselves, works of art. Early on this inclined towards what one critic called "a protest against the niggling detail, the factual accuracy of sharp all-over ordinary photography." "Concentration, strength, massing of light and shade, breadth of effect," he continued, "are the highly prized virtues."[52] Sometimes this led to deliberate blurring at the printing stage, or even — in the case of Stieglitz' friend Frank Eugene and others — to the use of pencil and paint on the negative. In effect, this "pictorialism" once more marked the assimiliation of photography toward painting.

But, despite Stieglitz' love of painting and his desire for the highest artistic status for photography, his deepest instincts led him in his own practice to become what Caffin termed "an exponent of the 'straight photograph,' working chiefly in the open air, with rapid exposure, leaving his models to pose themselves, and relying for results upon *means strictly photographic*."[53] Increasingly Stieglitz came to value those photographs — such as his own beautifully balanced view of some of a ship's complement of passengers in "The Steerage" (1907) — which proclaimed themselves as unmanipulated photographs rather than imitations of paintings, however lovely. In views from the window of 291, in studies of the hands of his second wife, painter Georgia O'Keeffe, in a series of cloud pictures he called "equivalents," he moved towards an expression and evocation of emotion strictly by the formal properties of organic and man-made objects as framed by the camera.[54] Not quite single-handedly, he thus established "straight photography" as the dominant tradition of American photography this century — indeed, so much so that the reputations of some of the more painterly of the Photo-Secession artists have been all but eclipsed by contemporary figures like Vroman or Hine whom we now recognise as exponents of the straight tradition and who went virtually unnoticed in artistic circles in Photo-Secession days.

The Variety of Genius

Despite the predominance of the straight tradition, other approaches did not entirely die out. In 1917 Ezra Pound's friend Alvin Langdon Coburn made his "Vortographs," abstracts deliberately created by photographing common objects reflected by three mirrors clamped together. Others printed part or all in negative, printed from several randomly superimposed negatives, made double or triple exposures, cropped negatives, engineered composite prints, and so on. In the twenties Man Ray produced his "Rayographs" and Lazlo Moholy-Nagy his "Photograms," but the straight approach became so indelibly associated with American endeavour in the medium that such other methods, even by major artists, were seen, literally, as peripheral — or even as part of some other medium.[55]

Nevertheless, while the influence of the straight tradition is obvious — for example, on the photographers of the FSA — many individual careers demonstrate a wide range of influence and approaches, though they may remain broadly within the dominant tradition. This is particularly true of Arnold Genthe, who was born in Germany, emigrated to the United States in 1896 and, before he became a naturalized American in 1918, had already acquired a sizeable reputation as a photographer. His career may appropriately be seen in the context of *both* pictorialism and the straight tradition.

His means of livelihood was the portrait studio, in his hands, especially in his earlier years in San Francisco, a kind of photographic salon where the rich, the celebrated — and, of course, the talented — came to converse and to sit for their likenesses. He achieved striking studies of such figures as musician Ignace Paderewski and writer Jack London by capturing them — as he put it in his autobiography — "in a carefully considered pattern of light and shade," using "soft tones," at an unexpected moment when he could bring out "essential features" rather than "unimportant detail."[56] But it could be argued that his claim to lasting recognition as a photographic artist has a firmer base in his work outside the confines of the studio — some of it unpremeditated, even haphazard, such as his oft-reproduced views of the aftermath of the same 1906 San Francisco earthquake that destroyed his own studio.

Even earlier, as his friend Will Irwin remembered, Genthe had frequented "the shadows and recesses of [San Francisco's] Chinatown," his "little camera half-hidden," searching out the exotic, more alien aspects of Chinese life — the seamed face of the merchant with his bodyguard, or "slave girls," or a line of children each hanging on to the pigtail of the preceding one. Shaemas O'Sheel, who wrote the preface for Genthe's *The Book of the Dance* (1916, 1920), with its reproductions of early colour photographs and other studies, believed that there was no "arrested motion" in such pictures, "but motion as it flows and is."[57] In fact, like those in *Isadora Duncan* (1929), although they have a flickering, half-seen quality which makes them seem ethereal, these views are rather static. There is a similar feel to his purposely blurred architectural studies of John D. Rockefeller's palatial home in *The Gardens of Kijkuit* (1919) and in the aptly named *Impressions of Old New Orleans* (1926).

Genthe's photographs were featured in Stieglitz' 1910 Buffalo

Arnold Genthe, *Firemen's Fight, San Francisco Earthquake*, 1906.
Published by permission of The Fine Arts Museum of San Francisco,
Aschenbach Foundation for Graphic Arts.

exhibition of pictorial work, and it is as if his years of collecting Japanese prints and his travels in the Orient gave him a consciously painterly outlook on photography, making him think of it as an art of large masses and delicate brush strokes. In this light, his earthquake views — houses like leaning towers on Sutter Street, or firemen spraying a building, a great snake of hosepipe almost arbitrarily filling the foreground (*see above*), or tents seen higgledy-piggledy in a refugee camp — possess a sharpness and a sheer presence that is sometimes lacking in the products of his more deliberate artistic aspirations.

f/64 — and Walker Evans

In 1932 the straight tradition was immeasurably strengthened by the formation on the West Coast of "Group f/64," membership of which included Ansel Adams, Imogen Cunningham and, most significantly, Edward Weston. They took that name because they habitually set their lenses at tiny apertures in order to get very detailed images and a high degree of definition over the whole of the field of vision, something the eye itself cannot do and the pictorialists had deliberately avoided.

In her seventy years as a photographer Imogen Cunningham did notable portraits — of "Martha Graham, Dancer" (1931), for instance, or "Gertrude Stein, Writer" (1937), or "Theodore Roethke,

Poet" (1959) — as well as landscapes, nudes, machines, and still lifes, the gamut of photographic subject-matter. But perhaps the work most akin to that of other f/64 members, especially Weston, was her marvellous *"Pflanzenformen,"* a series of vibrant plant studies done in the late twenties. In them the camera is very close, so that it is difficult to register scale, but it is not possible to mistake them for other forms.[58] In this there is a marked contrast with the ostensibly similar work by Edward Weston, his 1930 "Pepper No 30" (*see the Frontispiece*), say, or his "White Radish" (1933). Much of the power of Weston's images, despite his protestations to the contrary in his journals, his *Daybooks,* seems to lie in their capacity to act as visual metaphors: in the peppers a suggestion of naked human back and buttocks, in the radishes an insinuation of twisted human limbs. And in very many of his nudes there are intimations of massive land forms, and in his landscapes hints of humanity. Indeed, his camera caught things with such an intensity that his photographs seem a seamless series of archetypal images, constituting in their totality a vision of the very structure of the organic world.[59]

Until the f/64 group's dispersal in 1935, others, including Weston's son Brett, joined them, and the straight tradition was thereafter augmented by such camera workers as Wynn Bullock, Minor White, and Harry Callahan. Though, like Arnold Genthe, by no means a conscious member of any group or movement, the most celebrated exponent of the straight approach was, of course, Walker Evans.

His career — though he himself sometimes claimed otherwise — may be seen, despite its variety, as of a piece, and sewn with a conscious tightness. After his attachment to the FSA in the mid-thirties and *Fortune* magazine in the fifties, he spent his last years employed by Yale University to teach photography and aesthetics. He photographed in a number of regions of the United States and in several parts of the world, including Cuba and Great Britain. Over the years, he had associations with significant figures and movements in other arts, especially literature: the poet Hart Crane, for instance, the little magazine *Hound and Horn,* and James Agee, the novelist and film critic. In a life dedicated to photography, he worked with varying subject-matter: cityscapes, domestic interiors, advertising signs, portraits, industrial sites, and, in his mid-fifties series of plain, flat views of small hand tools — pliers, wrenches and the like — even still life of a sort.[60]

Evans' pictures are usually very still, quiet, composed, and sharply focussed; as William Stott put it, "he does not glimpse but frankly, interminably, stare."[61] But let us first consider certain of his images which seem, initially at least, untypical of his work as a whole: the 35mm portraits of New York subway riders published in *Many Are Called* (1941) and the 2¼ × 2¼" Detroit street portraits done in 1946. The subway passengers — a bewildering variety of American big-city characters — were taken unawares from a camera Evans concealed on his person as he sat on the opposite side of the subway car. They yawn, sleep, scratch, stare tragically into nothing, chat, echo each others' postures, sit in pairs but indicate separateness, dress differently or alike, think their own thoughts, look without realising they are looked at, are known and yet, ultimately, prove unknowable. The people captured in the Detroit images — some of them, at any rate, the more watchful perhaps — signal their awareness of the photographic process: they smile, half-smile, frown, or avert their eyes; though going somewhere, taken in mid-stride, they interact with the camera, move in another dimension towards it and, eventually, us. In both series, the illusion of picture depth is markedly limited by a flat background, the side of the subway carriage or a wall of stone in Detroit.[62] There is, thus, a high tension: between the severe two-dimensionality of the photograph and the strong intimation of otherness, of lives all their own, of time and its passage, of, indeed, the subject-matter.

In effect, then, these seemingly untypical works — done in series, too, which emphasizes movement and time — are deeply akin to Evans' classic still interiors totally void of people. The two-dimensionality indicates a degree of abstraction, at the least a tendency towards abstraction, while the signs of time and human action indicate a desire to capture reality directly, a search for realism. Of course, almost all photography — perhaps all art — exhibits this tension to some extent, as, in different forms, we have seen in the work of Curtis, Hine and Porter. But the supreme quality of Evans' pictures seems to depend upon the sheer frequency, force and variation with which he managed to display it — whether in views of clapboard frontages of tenant farmers' homes, the laden shelves of a country store, the "Ford Plant at River Rouge, Michigan" (1947), or "Robert Frank's Store, Nova Scotia" (1971).

One of the finest of his images is his 1935 "Coal Miner's House, Scott's Run, West Virginia" (*see the back cover of this pamphlet*). It depicts certain items of the house — an upended broom, a bent wood rocking chair and, less noticeable, a crowbar — against an interior wall of the house which has been decorated with large advertising hoardings, including a Father Christmas Coca Cola sign. Many viewers may be tempted to read the picture in sociological terms, as a set of social indicators: the crumpled cushion on the chair, the broken linoleum, the walls and ceiling patched or insulated with cardboard from cardboard boxes — all these speak of poverty, even desperation. On the other hand, the broom, say, certainly the chair, even the crowbar, are beautiful functional objects, testimony to the skills of man's hands . . . . Some viewers will be likely to sense a symbolic overtone in the photograph akin to that we observed in one of

Davidson's Harlem pictures: the Santa Claus figure seems to stand for a level of comfort and joy that is evident nowhere in the fabric of the house and, further, the other advertisement, showing a well-groomed couple in academic gowns above the words "BUY GRADUATION GIFTS HERE," hints at opportunities that the miner's material goods could not possibly purchase for his children. It is somewhat less easy to discern that these (possibly conflicting) readings — and, doubtless, others — are possible because of the recurrence of the collage-like two dimensionality that we have pinpointed elsewhere: it both offers the illusion of depth *(reality)* and denies it, seems instead a flat and somewhat bizarre *picture.*

As T.S. Eliot saw with reference to poetry, the past — and the future — are changed by the present. The values of the straight approach — usually, as here, not expressed with any marked analytical precision — were institutionalized in the photographic exhibitions and publications of the Museum of Modern Art. Probably the single most influential text was John Szarkowski's *The Photographer's Eye* (1966) in which the constituents of a way of seeing unique or distinctive to the camera were enunciated, and mostly illustrated by American examples. Szarkowski emphasized: "the thing itself," concentration on actuality; details, details perhaps observable only by the camera; the way that "the frame" determines meaning, in that the relationships between parts of the image within the frame have a force quite separate from any relationship their reference might or might not have had in reality; the importance of time, the manner in which a photograph both attests to the passing of time and, simultaneously, seems to freeze a particular moment; and, lastly, "the vantage point," often an unexpected one, from which the camera can be made to look.[63] Judged from this perspective, certain images by anonymous figures of the past — perhaps taken with no artistic intention at all — could be honoured, known but hitherto neglected photographers could be rescued from oblivion. Thus, such older artists as Frances Benjamin Johnston — together with many figures of somewhat more dubious stature — came to be located in the tradition.

In fact, the straight approach was so dominant that in the eyes of critics like Nathan Lyons, it came by the late sixties to seem a somewhat inhibiting orthodoxy that such figures as Jerry Uelsmann, Duane Michals and Robert Heinecken would need to subvert.[64] This they did — in the creation of gothic, absurd, or fantastical images, images that exhibit a troubled approximation to recognisable fragments of physical reality, but a highly attenuated reference, as if arisen from some subterranean dream domain or anti-world. At about the same time, to Susan Sontag *all* photography, whether "straight" or otherwise, was coming to seem surreal, and vexing.

Disturbing Portraits of America

The evolution of the artistic tradition in American photography was reflected within the genre of portraiture, in which Americans had so excelled in the nineteenth century. Many well-known twentieth-century photographers maintained this excellence, including Edward Steichen throughout his long career. In 1903 — by chance, he always insisted — he presented the financier J. Pierpont Morgan with his bullish head strikingly alert and his hand gripping a high-lit chair arm that looks remarkably like an unsheathed dagger. Steichen also framed Greta Garbo's flawless features in her own dark-clothed arms (1928) and lent Gloria Swanson's face an extra air of mystery by using an elaborate veil (1924). His younger contemporary, Paul Strand, made numerous fine portraits. Perhaps those first published in 1940 and reproduced in his *The Mexican Portfolio* (1967) are the most memorable: young men with the determined chins of so many Zapatas; people with the deep, timid eyes of peasants unacquainted with, perhaps, the evils of a complex world; a life-like wooden statue of Christ with the face of a Mexican villager below his crown of thorns, his body slightly leaning away (as if wincing) from the spiky leaves of a plant to the right.[65]

Arnold Newman specialized in portraying artists (including such photographers as Adams, Steichen and Strand) and tried to relate them to the characteristic forms of their own art. Pop artist Tom Wesselmann, for example, was captured wearing a hat which, in turn, was topped by an enormous female nipple, presumably belonging to one of his own "Great American Nude" series (1962-64); the photograph gives the impression that the nipple simultaneously emanates, so to speak, from Wesselmann's head and frames it, giving him definition and being. Marie Cosindas, meanwhile, exhibited a high degree of artistry and technical virtuosity by making colour portraits very early in the life of the instant polaroid process which gave both the sense of immediate intimacy that we might expect from such a medium *and* the quality of considered summation possessed by penetrating portraits in any medium; see, for instance, her 1965 rendering of radical political writer Max Eastman in his tranquil and conservative old age.[66]

Richard Avedon's best portraits — including his much reproduced "The Generals of the Daughters of the American Revolution" (c.1963) — were much less complimentary to his subjects, as the title of one of his books, *Nothing Personal* (1964), indicates. A number of critics expressed surprise that someone so devoted to very glossy and flattering fashion work for *Vogue* and the like could also cast such a cold eye on the physical appearance of his less glamorous subjects, however rich.[67] Such a disparity reached a new height in the work of Diane Arbus.

The posthumous exhibition of her photographs, held at New York's Museum of Modern Art in 1972, attracted more visitors than any previous show of a single photographer's work. Arbus, like Avedon, made her living as a fashion photographer, but her exhibition consisted of views of midgets, inhabitants of an asylum, members of two nudist colonies, transvestites, carnival troupers, assorted freaks, and other alienated and marginal individuals. These people are not caught in fleeting candid camera shots, unawares, as if by a peeping tom, or trying to hide the marks of their difference from the generality of human beings; instead, they appear relatively relaxed, present themselves frontally to the camera and, if anything, flaunt their flaws or signs of distinction. In other words, initially at least, these Arbus pictures seem a logical extension of the straight tradition. Moreover, Arbus' death by suicide soon after she became famous in the late sixties, appeared to provide additional testimony to their authenticity.

But a close examination of the photographs themselves can be disturbing — and not primarily because of their rather startling subject-matter. "Woman with fur collar on the street, New York City, 1968," for example, was taken *very* close, closer than our eyes would ever normally be to a total stranger; her face, its lines and ridges, thus assaults us. If it were not for this sense of enforced intimacy, she might well seem a perfectly ordinary, if somewhat overweight, middle-aged woman. Again, "A Puerto Rican housewife, New York City, 1963" was clearly taken from slightly below as the woman sat on her bed; we almost have to look *up* her legs; as her dress has a low neckline, this positioning suggests a sexual availability supposedly denied by the picture's caption. A low camera angle is also evident in "A Jewish giant at home with his parents in the Bronx, New York, 1970," and the garishness of the scene is further enhanced by the deep shadows thrown by the flash explosion on to the wall behind the ill-assorted trio. Indeed, so far from empathy with the rejected, there is, all told, something profoundly exploitative about these Arbus images. Unintentionally she herself put it well: ". . . there's a kind of power thing about the camera. I mean everybody knows you've got some edge . . . . It fixes them in a way."[68]

It was comments like this which partly prompted the writing of Susan Sontag's brilliant essay on Arbus for *The New York Review of Books* in 1973, an essay eventually incorporated in *On Photography*. Sontag was particularly perturbed by the limited range of subject-matter in Arbus' work:

> All her subjects are equivalent. And making equivalences between freaks, mad people, suburban couples, and nudists is a very powerful judgement, one in complicity with a recognisable political mood shared by many educated, left-liberal Americans. The subjects of Arbus' photographs are all members of

the same family, inhabitants of a single village. Only, as it happens, the idiot village is America. Instead of showing identity between things which are different (Whitman's democratic vista), everybody is shown to look the same.

The reference to Whitman was not accidental. Sontag viewed the progress of photography in America as the inevitable descendant of the earlier marriage of consumerism and technology to the Whitmanian imperative to see the beauty of the world in any "iota" of it, however trivial. There has been, she said, a decline from the Whitmanian ideal. Photographers could capture any aspect of life as a supposed exemplum of the whole but, as she put it, "without Whitman's delirious powers of synthesis, what they documented was discontinuity, detritus, loneliness, greed, sterility." The collection of assorted images, each with no significant meaning or relation to the others, was an act of surrealism to Sontag. "The best of American photography," she said,

> has given itself over to the consolations of Surrealism, and America has been discovered as the quintessential Surrealist country. It is obviously too easy to say that America is just a freak show, a wasteland . . . . What we have left of Whitman's discredited dream of cultural revolution are paper ghosts and a sharp-eyed witty program of despair.[69]

Underlying so much of Sontag's pessimism in *On Photography* is a justifiable questioning of photography's assumed ability to record reality itself; Sontag often sees the photographic image as an evasion, a substitute for actual human experience. The same charge could, of course, be levelled at all art forms — from the novel to the radio play — in that art is not, after all, life. Nevertheless, photography is, as we have seen, especially problematic. The fact that Sontag addressed the medium as seriously as this, questioned it as profoundly as this, was one way of marking its coming of age. Like the other American arts, photography has lost its innocence.

Guide to Further Reading
— and Viewing

The development of photography as a whole, and American contributions to it, are probably best covered in Beaumont Newhall's standard work *The History of Photography* (1939; 1982)[55]* and C.W. Ceram's *Archaeology of the Cinema* (1965).[9]* Robert Taft, *Photography and the American Scene* (1938; 1964),[11]* and Richard Rudisill, *Mirror Image* (1971),[20]* are particularly good on the relationship between photography and American society; also useful is William Welling, *Photography in America: The Formative Years, 1839-1900* (New York: Crowell, 1978). Collections of documents which both offer first-hand insights into the medium and complement the historical accounts are Beaumont Newhall, ed., *Photography: Essays and Images* (London: Secker and Warburg, 1980), and Vicki Goldberg, ed., *Photography in Print: Writings from 1816 to the Present* (New York: Simon and Schuster, 1981).

The works devoted to particular phases or kinds of American photography vary enormously in scope and quality, but the following can be fully recommended. For photography in and of the West, see Weston J. Naef and James N. Wood, *Era of Exploration: The Rise of Landscape Photography in the West, 1860-85* (Boston: New York Graphic Society, 1975); Karen and William Current, *Photography and the Old West* (New York: Harry Abrams, 1978); and two books by Ralph W. Andrews, *Picture Gallery Pioneers* (Seattle: Superior, 1964) and *Photographers of the Frontier West* (Seattle: Superior, and New York: Bonanza, 1965). For the Photo-Secession era, see Robert Doty, *Photo-Secession* (1960)[52] and Weston J. Naef, *The Collection of Alfred Stieglitz* (New York: Viking, 1978). For the f/64 movement, see Beaumont Newhall's chapter on "Straight Photography" in his *History* and Nancy Newhall, *Ansel Adams* (1963), pp.65-80.[24] For photography in the thirties, especially the FSA Unit, see William Stott, *Documentary Expression and Thirties America* (1973),[61] F. Jack Hurley, *Portrait of a Decade: Roy Stryker and the Development of Documentary Photography in the Thirties* (Baton Rouge: Louisiana State UP, 1972), and Roy Emerson Stryker and Nancy Wood, *In this Proud Land: America, 1935-1943, as seen in the FSA Photographs* (Greenwich, Conn.: New York Graphic Society, 1973). For photojournalism, see Arthur Rothstein, *Photojournalism* (1956; rev. edn., Garden City, N.Y.: Amphoto, 1982) and — for approaches rather than facts — Harold Evans, *Pictures on a Page* (London: Heinemann, 1978). For portraiture, see Ben Maddow's massive *Faces* (Boston: New York Graphic Society, 1977).

For full bibliographical details, see the appropriate reference in the Notes, as indicated.

The images of photography constitute data which needs to be interpreted, understood and, sometimes, appreciated, even loved. For interesting attempts to come to terms with the medium, besides Susan Sontag's *On Photography* (1977)[3] and Roland Barthes' *Camera Lucida* (1981),[3] see Paul Hill and Thomas Cooper, eds., *Dialogue with Photography* (London: Thames and Hudson, 1979), Van Deren Coke, ed., *One Hundred Years of Photographic History: Essays in Honor of Beaumont Newhall* (Albuquerque: University of New Mexico Press, 1975), and James Enyeart, Robert D. Monroe and Philip Stokes, *Three Classic American Photographs: Texts and Contexts* (University of Exeter, American Arts Pamphlet No.7, 1982). As an aid, especially with reference to art photography, the words of the image makers themselves are often invaluable; see Nathan Lyons, ed., *Photographers on Photography* (1966),[8] James Danziger and Barnaby Conrad III, eds., *Interviews with Master Photographers* (New York and London: Paddington Press, 1977), and Margaretta K. Mitchell, ed., *Recollections: Ten Women of Photography* (New York: Viking, 1979). For good selections from notable journals of the past, see Jonathan Green, ed., *Camera Work: A Critical Anthology* (Millerton, N.Y.: Aperture, 1973), and *Life: The First Decade, 1936-1945* (Boston: New York Graphic Society, 1979).

Readers concerned to dig deeper will find that photography — perhaps because it overlaps with so many other fields, from painting to chemistry — is fortunate in its reference provision. Full-scale bibliographical works are Albert Boni, ed., *Photographic Literature*, 2 vols. (Hastings, N.Y.: Morgan and Morgan, 1962 and 1972) and the fine photography section, compiled by Beaumont Newhall, of Barnard Karpel, ed., *Arts in America: A Bibliography*, 4 vols. (Washington, D.C.: Smithsonian Institution, 1979). There is no fully satisfactory up-to-date encyclopaedia of American photography, but many libraries contain Willard D. Morgan, ed., *The Encyclopaedia of Photography*, 20 vols. (New York: Greystone Press, 1963-64) and photography receives good treatment in *The Britannica Encyclopaedia of American Art* (New York: Simon and Schuster, 1973). See also the excellent Time-Life Library of Photography, 17 vols. (New York: Time-Life Books, 1971-72), and the authoritative biographical guide edited by Colin Naylor et al., *Contemporary Photographers* (London: Macmillan, 1982). These works cover aspects of the subject not treated in this pamphlet, like film still work and fashion, advertising or war photography.

In all consideration of photography, there is no substitute for actually viewing, even handling, the images themselves. Most state historical societies and important art museums in the United States have files of relevant photographs for both exhibition and research and will provide inexpensive prints. The beginnings of union catalogues are to be found in James McQuaid, ed., *An Index of American Photographic Collections* (Boston: G.K. Hall, 1982) and — for Britain, including Americana — John Wall, ed., *Directory of British Photographic Collections* (London: Heinemann, 1977). Of various guides to major collections, note especially Paul Vanderbilt, ed., *Guide to the Special Collections of Prints and Photographs in the Library of Congress* (Washington, D.C.: Library of Congress, 1955). Whole collections are now becoming accessible in microform: for example, Chadwyck-Healey publish all the quarter of a million FSA prints in microfilm, and University Microfilms International have brought out *Photographic Views of New York City*, 54,000 photographs from the New York Public Library. The numerous compilations derived from these vast archives include *The American Image* (1979),[15] based on the National Archives, and *American Album* (1968).[13] On limited topics, some compilations are remarkably good, notably Allon Schoener, ed., *Portal to America: The East Side, 1870-1925* (New York: Holt, Rinehart and Winston, 1967), and, for "traditional" images of Native Americans, especially in the Pacifiic Northwest, Ralph W. Andrews, *Indian Primitive* (Seattle: Superior, 1960).

For first-hand experience of photographs small travelling exhibitions are a rich resource. In the United States, the Smithsonian Institution's Traveling Exhibition Service (SITES) is responsible for a number of photographic shows (usually marked by excellent catalogues), as are other major museum services. In Britain, exhibitions of American photographs are available from the Photographer's Gallery and the Victoria and Albert Museum, London; Impressions Gallery, York; The John Judkyn Memorial, Freshford Manor, Bath; and the Audio-Visual Unit, the University of Exeter Library, Exeter. Many photographs are also available in slide form; a principal supplier is Light Impressions Corporation, PO Box 3012, Photo Slide and AV Dept., Rochester, New York 14614. A particularly good set of approximately 2,000 slides is *The American History Slide Collection* available from Instructional Resources Corporation, 12121 Dove Circle, Laurel, Maryland 20811. British secondary school teachers may borrow such slides from the American Studies Resources Centre, Polytechnic of Central London, including an excellent slide set compiled for the Centre by William Stott: *Lewis Hine and American Social Photography, 1904-36* (1982).

Notes

1. Michael Lesy, *Wisconsin Death Trip* (N.Y.: Pantheon, 1973), in which the photographs were sometimes doctored by Lesy; David Galloway, *A Family Album* (London: Calder, 1978); Paul Theroux, *Picture Palace* (Harmondsworth: Penguin, 1981).

2. Marshall McLuhan, *Understanding Media: The Extensions of Man* (N.Y.: McGraw-Hill, 1964); William F. Ivins, *Prints and Visual Communication* (1953; reprint ed., Cambridge, Mass., and London: MIT, 1968), which has since been superseded by Estelle Jussim, *Visual Communication and the Graphic Arts: Photographic Technologies in the Nineteenth Century* (N.Y.: Bowker, 1974).

3. Susan Sontag, *On Photography* (Harmondsworth: Penguin, 1979); Roland Barthes, *Camera Lucida: Reflections on Photography* (London: Cape, 1982).

4. See M. Gidley, "The History of Photography in the Context of American Studies," in Margaret Harker, ed., *Proceedings of the European Society for the History of Photography, 1981* (Antwerpen: Provincial Museum of Photography, 1982), 33-38.

5. See William Culp Darrah, *The World of Stereographs* (Gettysburg, Pa.: Darrah, 1977) and Edward W. Earle, ed., *Points of View: The Stereograph in America — A Cultural History* (Rochester, N.Y.: Visual Studies Workshop, 1979).

6. Robert Bartlett Haas, *Muybridge: Man in Motion* (Berkeley, Los Angeles and London: Univ. of California Press, 1976).

7. Reese V. Jenkins, *Images and Enterprise: Technology and the American Photographic Industry* (Baltimore and London: Johns Hopkins UP, 1976).

8. Paul Strand, "Photography and the New God" (1922), in Nathan Lyons, ed., *Photographers on Photography* (Englewood Cliffs, N.J.: Prentice-Hall, 1966), pp.138-44.

9. C.W. Ceram, *Archaeology of the Cinema* (N.Y.: Harcourt Brace, 1965), p.16.

10. Conor Cruise O'Brien, in *New York Review of Books,* **15,** No.8 (5 Nov. 1970), 12.

11. Lincoln quoted in Robert Taft, *Photography and the American Scene* (1938; N.Y.: Dover, 1964), p.195. See also James D. Horan, *Matthew Brady: Historian with a Camera* (New York: Crown, 1955).

12. For Caesar, see Peter J. Parish's BAAS pamphlet, *Slavery,* p.25; and, for Kinsey, see Darius and Tabitha Kinsey, *Kinsey Photographer: A Half Century of Negatives,* 2 vols. (San Francisco: Scrimshaw, 1975). See also Murray Morgan, *One Man's Gold Rush: A Klondike Album: Photographs by E.A Hegg* (Seattle and London: Washington UP, 1967); John Szarkowski, *E.J. Bellocq: Storyville Portraits* (N.Y.: Museum of Modern Art, 1970).

13. Oliver Jensen, Joan Paterson Kerr, Murray Belsky, *American Album* (N.Y.: American Heritage, 1968).

14. See John Kouwenhoven, "American Studies: Words or Things," in Marshall Fishwick, ed., *American Studies in Transition* (Philadelphia: Pennsylvania UP, 1964), pp.15-35.

15. Alan Trachtenberg, *The American Image* (N.Y.: Pantheon, 1979).

16. Robert A. Weinstein and Larry Booth, *The Collection, Use and Care of Historical Photographs* (Nashville: American Association for State and Local History, 1977), p.3.

17. Both Grabill photographs are reproduced in Alan Fern, Milton Kaplan, et al., *Viewpoints: A Selection from the Pictorial Collections of the Library of Congress* (Washington, DC: Library of Congress, 1975), pp.45, 122-23.

18. Roland Barthes, *Image, Music, Text* (London: Fontana, 1977), p.27.

19. Reproduced in Earle, ed., *Points of View,* p.47.

20. Richard Rudisill, *Mirror Image: The Influence of the Daguerreotype on American Society* (Albuqerque: Univ. of New Mexico Press, 1971).

21. Sontag, *On Photography,* p.65.

22. M. Gidley, *With One Sky Above Us: Life on an Indian Reservation at the Turn of the Century: Photographs by E.H. Latham* (N.Y.: Putnam's Sons,1979).

23. See James D. Horan, *Timothy O'Sullivan: America's Forgotten Photographer* (Garden City, N.Y.: Doubleday, 1966), p.169.

24. S.R. Frankel, in *Artnews*, **80** (1981), 98-99. See Liliane de Cock, ed., *Ansel Adams* (Hastings, N.Y.: Morgan and Morgan, 1972), and Nancy Newhall, *Ansel Adams: The Eloquent Light* (San Francisco: Sierra Club, 1963).

25. Reproduced, among other places, in John Szarkowski, ed., *The Photographer and the American Landscape* (N.Y.: Museum of Modern Art, 1963), p.11.

26. M. Gidley, ed., *The Vanishing Race: Selections from E.S. Curtis' "The North American Indian"* (N.Y.: Taplinger, 1977). For Vroman, see William Webb and Robert A. Weinstein, *Dwellers at the Source: Southwestern Indian Photographs of A.C. Vroman, 1895-1904* (N.Y.: Grossman, 1973).

27. Alexander Alland, *Jacob A. Riis: Photographer and Citizen* (London: Gordon Fraser, 1975), p.11.

28. Robert H. Bremner, *From the Depths: The Discovery of Poverty in the United States* (N.Y.: New York UP, 1956), p.69. *How the Other Half Lives* has been reprinted, with fewer photographs (N.Y.: Dover, 1971). For the complexities of "Progressive" attitudes, see J.A. Thompson's BAAS Pamphlet, *Progressivism*.

29. *Men at Work* (1932; reprint, N.Y.: Dover, 1977). See also Alan Trachtenberg, et al., *America and Lewis Hine: Photographs, 1904-1940* (Millerton, N.Y.: Aperture, 1977); Judith Mara Gutman, *Lewis W. Hine* (N.Y.: Grossman, 1974).

30. Barthes, *Camera Lucida*, p.51.

31. See Arthur Rothstein, *The Depression Years* (N.Y.: Dover, 1978); Robert L. Snyder, *Pare Lorentz and the Documentary Film* (Norman: Oklahoma UP, 1968), which also demonstrates the pervasiveness of ideas akin to Stryker's.

32. Sean Callahan, ed., *The Photographs of Margaret Bourke-White* (London: Secker & Warburg, 1973).

33. Thomas H. Garver, ed., *Just Before the War: Urban America from 1935 to 1941 as seen by Photographers of the FSA* (Balboa, Cal.: Newport Harbor Art Museum, 1968), n.p.

34. Interview with the author, August 1980. For Collier's later work, see his *The Awakening Valley* (Chicago UP, 1949) and *Visual Anthropology: Photography as a Research Method* (N.Y.: Holt, Rinehart and Winston, 1967).

35. See Gordon Parks, *Moments Without Proper Names* (London: Secker and Warburg, 1975); D. Lange, *Dorothea Lange* (N.Y.: Museum of Modern Art, 1966); and Davis Pratt, ed., *The Photographic Eye of Ben Shahn* (Cambridge, Mass., and London: Harvard UP, 1975).

36. W.E. Smith, "Photographic Journalism" (1948), in Lyons, *Photographers on Photography*, pp.102-05; and W.E. Smith, *W. Eugene Smith: His Photographs and Notes* (N.Y.: Aperture, 1969).

37. Bruce Davidson, *East 100th Street* (Cambridge, Mass.: Harvard UP, 1970); Robert Frank, *The Americans* (1959; rev. edn., N.Y.: Aperture, 1969).

38. Sontag, *On Photography*, p.105.

39. Richard Pare, ed., *Court House: A Photographic Document* (N.Y.: Horizon, 1978).

40. Vanderbilt's photographs appear in Szarkowski's *The Photographer and the American Landscape;* and the younger photographers' in idem, *Mirrors and Windows: American Photography Since 1960* (N.Y.: Museum of Modern Art, 1978).

41. Lee Friedlander, *The American Monument* (N.Y.: Eakins Foundation, 1976), the prints in which may be removed for exhibition purposes.

42. Friedlander, *Self-Portrait* (New City, N.Y.: Haywire, 1970) and *Photographers* (ibid., 1978).

43. Robert A. Sobieszek and Odette M. Appel, eds., *The Spirit of Fact: The Daguerreotypes of Southworth and Hawes, 1843-1862* (Boston: Godine, 1976).

44. Quoted in Harold F. Pfister, *Facing the Light: Historic American Portrait Daguerreotypes* (Washington, D.C.: Smithsonian Institution, 1978), p.149, which also reproduces fine daguerreotypes of most of the figures mentioned here.

45. Horace Traubel, *With Whitman in Camden* (Boston: Small, Maynard, 1906), p.367; Whitman, *Leaves of Grass* (1855), eds. Harold W. Blodgett and Sculley Bradley (London UP, 1968), pp.200, 300. See also Gay Wilson Allen, ed., *The Artisitic Legacy of Walt Whitman* (N.Y.: New York UP, 1970), pp.127-52.

46. Edward Weston, *Leaves of Grass by Walt Whitman* (1942; reprint ed., N.Y. and London: Paddington, 1976).

47. Gleason pictures from such works as his *Through the Year With Thoreau* (1917) are most accessible in Henry D. Thoreau, *The Illustrated Walden* (Princeton, N.J.: Princeton UP, 1973).

48. Wright Morris, *The Inhabitants* (1946; 2nd ed., N.Y.: Da Capo, 1972); Sherwood Anderson and Art Sinsabaugh, *Six Mid-American Chants* (Highlands, N.C.: Jonathan Williams, 1964).

49. Eliot Porter, *In Wilderness is the Preservation of the World* (San Francisco: Sierra Club, 1962).

50. Elizabeth Lindquist-Cock, *The Influence of Photography on American Landscape Painting, 1839-1880* (N.Y.: Garland, 1977).

51. See William Innes Homer, *Alfred Stieglitz and the American Avant-Garde* (Boston: New York Graphic Society, 1977).

52. Quoted in Robert Doty, *Photo-Secession: Photography as a Fine Art* (Rochester, N.Y.: George Eastman House, 1960), p.24.

53. Ibid., p.17. Emphasis added.

54. Doris Bry, *Alfred Stieglitz: Photographer* (Boston: Museum of Fine Arts, 1965); Dorothy Norman, *Alfred Stieglitz: An American Seer* (Millerton, N.Y.: Aperture, 1973).

55. For those approaches, see Beaumont Newhall, *A History of Photography from 1839 to the Present Day* (1939; 5th edn., N.Y.: Museum of Modern Art, 1982), ch. on "The Quest for Form." For Coburn, see Malcolm Bradbury's BAAS Pamphlet, *The Expatriate Tradition in Amercan Literature*, p.14.

56. Arnold Genthe, *As I Remember* (N.Y.: Reynal and Hitchcock, 1936), p.261.

57. Genthe, *Pictures of Old Chinatown* (N.Y.: Moffat, Yard, 1908), p.3 and *The Book of the Dance* (Boston: International Publisherrs, 1920), p.xvi.

58. Margery Mann, ed., *Imogen Cunningham: Photographs* (Seattle and London: Univ. of Washington Press, 1970).

59. Nancy Newhall, ed., *The Daybooks of Edward Weston*, 2 vols. (Millerton, N.Y.: Aperture, 1973); Ben Maddow, *Edward Weston: Fifty Years* (ibid., 1973).

60. See the excellent selection, *Walker Evans: First and Last* (London: Secker and Warburg, 1978); also Walker Evans, *American Photographs* (N.Y.: Museum of Modern Art, 1938), and Lesley K. Baier, *Walker Evans at "Fortune", 1945-65* (Wellesley, Mass.: Wellesley College Museum, 1977).

61. William Stott, *Documentary Expression and Thirties America* (N.Y.: Oxford UP, 1973), p.268.

62. For Evans' aesthetic, see Mike Weaver, "Walker Evans: Magic Realist," *Creative Camera* (September 1977), 292-94.

63. John Szarkowski, *The Photographer's Eye* (N.Y.: Museum of Modern Art, 1966), pp.6-12.

64. Nathan Lyons, *The Persistence of Vision* (N.Y.: Horizon, 1967), which, like Szarkowski's *Mirrors and Windows*, contains work by Uelsmann and others.

65. Edward Steichen, *A Life in Photography* (Garden City, N.Y.: Doubleday, 1963); Paul Strand, *The Mexican Portfolio* (N.Y.: Da Capo, 1967), and *Paul Strand: Sixty Years of Photographs* (Millerton, N.Y.: Aperture, 1976).

66. Arnold Newman, *Artists: Portraits from Four Decades* (London: Weidenfeld and Nicolson, 1980); Marie Cosindas, *Color Photographs* (Boston: New York Graphic Society, 1978).

67. Richard Avedon, *Nothing Personal*, with an Introduction by James Baldwin (Harmondsworth and Baltimore: Penguin, 1964).

68. Doon Arbus and Marvin Israel, eds., *Diane Arbus: Photographs* (Millerton, N.Y.: Aperture, 1972), p.13.

69. Sontag, *On Photography*, pp.47, 48.

BAAS PAMPHLETS IN AMERICAN STUDIES

*Pamphlets may be purchased from BAAS Pamphlets, c/o The Historical Association,
59a Kennington Park Road, London SE11 4JH, England.*